Interactive Bible Study Bulletin Boards

48 Hands-On Bulletin Boards with Mini-Lessons

by Lynette Pyne

Carson-Dellosa Publishing Company
Greensboro, North Carolina

It is the mission of Carson-Dellosa Christian Publishing to create the highest-quality Scripture-based children's products that teach the Word of God, share His love and goodness, assist in faith development, and glorify His Son, Jesus Christ.

"... *teach me your ways so I may know you.* ... "
Exodus 33:13

Credits

Editor: .... Sabena Maiden
Inside Illustrations: ... Darcy Bell-Myers
Cover Design: .... Annette Hollister-Papp
Colorization: .... Mark Conrad
Layout Design: .... Mark Conrad
Cover Illustrations: ... Ron Kauffman

Scripture taken from the HOLY BIBLE, NEW INTERNATIONAL VERSION Copyright © 1973, 1978, 1984 International Bible Society. Used by permission of Zondervan Bible Publishers.

ISBN 1-59441-076-3

Table of Contents

Bulletin boards provide a wonderful method not only to present a story or concept in a vivid way, but they can also be used as ongoing teaching tools. Once posted for display, you may teach the initial lesson, then as you delve further into an idea, you can refer your students to the bulletin board to point out new ideas and convenient reminders. This book contains 48 complete bulletin board ideas from the Old and New Testaments to teach a variety of stories, lessons, and themes from the Bible. For each bulletin board, there is a list of Reference Verses to show from where the bulletin board idea came, a Key Bible Verse to tie in the bulletin board's message, a short Mini-Lesson to present the message, a complete *Materials Needed* list, and easy-to-follow assembly instructions with sample text where appropriate.

It is recommended that before you teach each bulletin board lesson, begin by reading the applicable Scripture using the listed *Reference Verses*. Each bulletin board can be made with your students by following the detailed assembly instructions. A suggested background color and title, a page number for the corresponding patterns, and the full-color illustration for each bulletin board make creating your own vibrant displays fun and easy. The materials that are needed to complete the bulletin boards are items you likely already have in your classroom—butcher paper, scissors, glue, crayons, markers, construction paper, and other basic craft materials. It's also quite simple to personalize your displays by adding a coordinating border, cutting out the title from fabric strips, or adding other special touches. You and your students will enjoy making these interactive creations, as well as learn many valuable lessons from God's Word.

Reference Verses
Genesis 1:1-31

Key Bible Verse
How many are your works, O Lord! In wisdom you made them all; the earth is full of your creatures. Psalm 104:24

Mini-Lesson
God created the heavens, oceans, land, plants, animals, and people. We see and understand God's power through the wonderful things He created. Honor God by caring for the earth He made for us. By respecting our environment, we can show God how much we love and admire His work! What are some things you can do to show your appreciation and love for God's world?

Materials Needed
Light-colored butcher paper, Creation picture and seven number patterns (p. 53-55), scissors, glue, white paper squares, hook-and-loop fasteners, crayons or markers, black marker, poster board

Assembly
Cover the bulletin board with light-colored butcher paper. Copy and cut out the six Creation picture patterns and seven number patterns. Glue each number pattern to the center of a white paper square, then write the corresponding Bible verse excerpts (if desired) onto each square (Genesis 1:3, 6, 9, 14, 20, 24 and 26, Genesis 2:2). Attach a hook-and-loop-fastener on the back of each Creation picture pattern and white paper square, then place the matching hook-and-loop fasteners in four rows on the bulletin board. Divide the class into small groups and give each group a verse and matching picture. Let students color the pictures. Create a quilt by having students attach the verses and pictures in the correct order onto the bulletin board. For the seventh verse, provide three blank squares for students to illustrate God's wonderful world. Use black marker to draw "stitch marks." Glue the illustrations beside the verse. Highlight the title by cutting out an arc from poster board and add the text.

Reference Verses
Genesis 1:26-31, 2:4-25

Key Bible Verse
Then God said, "Let us make man in our image, in our likeness, and let them rule over the fish of the sea and the birds of the air, over the livestock, over all the earth, and over all the creatures that move along the ground." Genesis 1:26

Mini-Lesson
Just like Adam and Eve, God created all of us and made each of us into a unique person. God knows all about you and has special plans for you. God wants us to love Him and follow His teachings. Be proud of the unique talents and gifts that God gave you!

Materials Needed
Two different colors of bright-colored butcher paper, scissors, black marker, picture frame pattern (p. 56), crayons or markers, sequins, stickers, glitter, glue, red, blue, and yellow construction paper

Assembly
Cover the bulletin board with bright-colored butcher paper. Cut a shorter piece of another bright-colored butcher paper and post it on top of the other butcher paper. Copy and cut out copies of the picture frame pattern. Inside each frame, write a letter from the title of the bulletin board. Mount the title in the center of the board. Write the remaining words using a black marker. Give each student a copy of the picture frame pattern. Let each students draw a self-portrait in the frame, then label it with her name and with a special phrase about herself. Provide markers, sequins, stickers, glitter, and glue to decorate the frames. Post the frames around the bulletin board. Accent with student-made heart cutouts made from red, blue, and yellow construction paper.

God's Promises

Reference Verses
Genesis 6:1-9:7

Key Bible Verse
God is our refuge and strength, an ever-present help in trouble. Psalm 46:1

Mini-Lesson
Noah trusted God and followed His instructions—even when those around him thought he was a bit strange. But Noah knew that if he listened to God, he and his family would be safe. Although people may sometimes let you down, you can always trust God. He has promised to care for you and He will. Can you think of a time when God helped you?

Materials Needed
Light blue butcher paper, brown butcher paper, white paper, ark section patterns (p. 57-58), Noah and dove with branch patterns (p. 59), crayons or markers, scissors, construction paper

Assembly
Cover the top three-fourths of the bulletin board with light blue butcher paper to resemble the sky. Cover the bottom fourth of the board with brown butcher paper to resemble land. Cut out clouds from white paper and post on the bulletin board. Divide the class into small groups and provide each with one of the ark section patterns. Have students color and cut out the ark section patterns. Let them "build" the ark by attaching the ark sections to the bulletin board. Give students markers, and have them trace their hands on construction paper to make several handprint patterns. On each of his handprint patterns, have the student write an example of when God has helped him. Then, have the student write a prayer of thanks on another handprint pattern. Create a rainbow above the completed ark using the handprint patterns, showing the many ways God has helped the class along with the student prayers of thanks (if desired). Accent the display using enlarged and colored copies of Noah and the dove with branch patterns.

Reference Verses
Genesis 15:1-6, 17:1-8, 15-17, 21:1-7

Key Bible Verse
Then you will know that I am the LORD; those who hope in me will not be disappointed. Isaiah 49:23

Mini-Lesson
Abraham and Sarah wished for a baby, and God promised to help them. God has control over our lives and will help us if we believe and have hope that He will do what is best for us. What good things do you hope God has in store for you?

Materials Needed
dark blue butcher paper, Abraham pattern (p. 60), crayons or markers, scissors, star patterns (p. 59-60), yellow paper

Assembly
Cover the bulletin board with dark blue butcher paper to resemble the night sky. Enlarge, color, and cut out the Abraham pattern. Display the pattern on the board. Copy several star patterns on yellow paper. On each star, write a question about the story of God's promise to Abraham (see Sample Text). For each question, leave a blank star for students to write the answers. Post the questions on the board. Divide the class into small groups and assign each group a question to answer and provide them a blank star to write it. Use the display to talk about how God keeps His promises to us.

Sample Text
• Why did Abraham think he wouldn't have a child? *He was 100 years old.*
• What does the name "Abraham" mean? *father of many nations*
• What did God promise Abraham? *many relatives*
• What did Abraham ask God for? *a baby*
• What did Sarah and Abraham name their son? *Isaac*

Reference Verses
Genesis 37-45

Key Bible Verse
Bear with each other and forgive whatever grievances you may have against one another. Forgive as the Lord forgave you. Colossians 3:13

Mini-Lesson
Joseph forgave his brothers, even though they treated him unkindly. Although apologizing can be hard sometimes, it can be even harder to forgive someone who has hurt your feelings. Remember that no matter what you do, God will forgive you if you ask Him. We should forgive others as God forgives us.

Materials Needed
Red, orange, yellow light green, dark green, light blue, dark blue, and purple butcher paper, Joseph pattern (p. 61), crayons or markers, scissors, coat pattern (p. 62), fabric scraps, shirt pattern (p. 62), glue, paper plates, yarn, stapler

Assembly
Cover the bulletin board with rounded strips of red, orange, yellow, light green, dark green, light blue, dark blue, and purple butcher paper to resemble a rainbow. Enlarge and cut out the Joseph pattern. Provide crayons or markers and let students decorate Joseph's coat with colorful designs. Post the pattern in the center of the display. Give each child a copy of the coat pattern. Provide fabric scraps for students to decorate their coats. Give each student a copy of the shirt pattern to cut out. Then, have students glue their coat patterns on top of their shirt patterns. Have students fold back the coat (by cutting the center seam) and write about forgiveness on the shirt patterns underneath. Provide paper plates for each student to draw a self-portrait, using yarn for hair. Staple the self-portrait plates above each coat pattern. As you talk about forgiveness, open each coat to reveal each student's thoughts.

Reference Verses
Exodus 2:1-10

Key Bible Verse
Trust in the L ORD *with all your heart and lean not on your own understanding.* Proverbs 3:5

Mini-Lesson
God protected Moses, for He had a special plan for him. God had great things in store for Moses, as He does for each of us. Know that you are precious to the Lord. Trust that He will protect you and keep you safe.

Materials Needed
Brown butcher paper, scissors, blue-green butcher paper, cattail pattern (p. 63), green construction paper, brown construction paper, toilet tissue tubes, stapler, brown chenille craft sticks, Miriam and Pharaoh's daughter patterns (p. 63), crayons or markers, baby Moses pattern (p. 63), basket pattern (p. 64), hook-and-loop fasteners

Assembly
Cover the bulletin board with brown butcher paper to resemble the ground. Cut a river from blue-green butcher paper and attach it across the display. Make several copies of the cattail patterns on green construction paper. Attach brown construction paper pieces around tubes and staple one at the top of each pattern to make a cattail. Add a brown chenille craft stick to the top. Post the cattails along the river. Enlarge, cut out, and color the Miriam and Pharaoh's daughter patterns. Place Miriam at the top of the river and Pharaoh's daughter at the bottom. Enlarge, cut out, color, and post a copy of the baby Moses pattern near Pharaoh's daughter. Make several copies of the basket pattern. On each pattern, write story details (see Sample Text). Attach a piece of hook-and-loop fastener to the back of each basket and its matching piece on the river. Have students place the patterns in order to tell the story of baby Moses.

Sample Text
• Moses placed in the basket by his mother.
• His sister Miriam watched over him.
• Pharaoh's daughter goes to the river.
• Moses is found by Pharaoh's daughter.

Reference Verses
Exodus 3:1-4:17

Key Bible Verse
I can do everything through him who gives me strength. Philippians 4:13

Mini-Lesson
Moses felt discouraged because he didn't think he could do what God asked of him. Sometimes we are called upon to do difficult tasks, but we can do them with God's help. When a tough challenge comes your way, remember that God can give you the strength to accomplish it. Just ask Him.

Materials Needed
Blue butcher paper, green butcher paper, Moses pattern (p. 65), crayons or markers, scissors, cloud and burning bush patterns (p. 64), red, orange, and yellow tissue paper, paintbrushes, glue thinned with water

Assembly
Cover the top of the bulletin board with blue butcher paper to resemble the sky and use green butcher paper to cover the bottom of the bulletin board to resemble a sloping hill. Enlarge, color, and cut out the Moses pattern. Post the pattern on the display. Copy and cut out the cloud pattern. Inside the cloud, write God said, "I will be with you." Post the cloud on the display. Give each child a copy of the burning bush pattern to cut out. Provide squares of red, orange, and yellow tissue paper. Allow students to use paintbrushes and thinned glue to attach the tissue paper to the burning bush patterns. When the glue has dried on the patterns, have each student write a positive message they can use when something seems too difficult (if desired). Attach the patterns to the board and use them as a reminder for students to never give up on God.

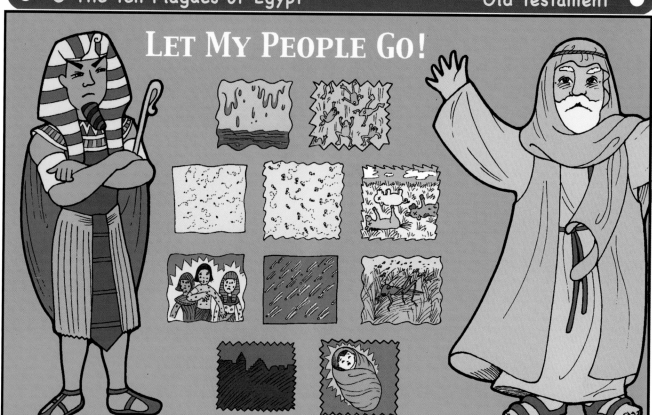

Reference Verses
Exodus 6-12

Key Bible Verse
But those who suffer he delivers in their suffering; he speaks to them in their affliction. Job 36:15

Mini-Lesson
God used the plagues against Egypt to show His power and might to Pharaoh. Each time Pharaoh refused to listen to God's Word, God's power was shown more and the plagues became more serious. Respect God's power and strength and obey His Word.

Materials Needed
Muted-colored butcher paper, Moses pattern (p. 65), Pharaoh pattern (p. 66), crayons or markers, scissors, the plague patterns (p. 66-68), poster board, hook-and-loop fasteners

Assembly
Cover the bulletin board with muted-colored butcher paper. Enlarge, color, and cut the Moses and Pharaoh patterns. Post Pharaoh on the left side of the board and Moses on the right side of the bulletin board. Enlarge, cut out, and color each of the plague patterns. Mount the patterns on poster board and cut them out. Trace each pattern on the board in sequential order. Attach pieces of hook-and-loop fastener to the back of each pattern and to the traced images on the bulletin board. Have students place the plagues in order, starting at Pharaoh and leading to Moses. Point out that the plagues became more severe as Pharaoh's heart hardened against God. Talk about how the most serious plague finally convinced Pharaoh to let the Israelites leave Egypt with Moses. Pharaoh could no longer deny God's awesome power.

PASSOVER

The pharaoh would not let the Israelites leave Egypt, even after the plagues had been sent by God. Finally, when the pharaoh's firstborn was struck down, he set Moses' people free.

When the plague of the first-born struck Egypt, God gave special commands to the Isrealites. Each family was to kill a lamb at twilight, then put blood from the lamb on their door frames. god would "passover" these homes and the children would be safe.

In remembrance of Passover, the Isrealites were to eat the roasted lamb meat with bitter herbs and bread made without yeast. The feast was to be held each year as a reminder of the Lord's passover.

Moses led 600,000 Israelites out of Egypt. God guided them through the desert and to the Red Sea. The pharoh's army chased them to the sea, but God parted the waters so the Isrealites could cross. The waters closed over the pharoh's army.

Reference Verses
Exodus 11-12

Key Bible Verse
...he saved us, not because of righteous things we had done, but because of his mercy.
Titus 3:5

Mini-Lesson
In this story, God shows how if we trust and follow Him, He will protect us. Just as God gave specific instructions to help the Israelites, he can save you too. Trust in the fact that God will help you.

Materials Needed
Four colors of bright butcher paper, Pharaoh pattern (p. 66), Moses pattern (p. 65), Passover plate and lamb patterns (p. 68), crayons or markers, scissors, glue

Assembly
Cover each quarter of the bulletin board with a different color of bright butcher paper. Use a marker to divide the display into four distinct colored sections. Enlarge and cut out the Pharaoh, Moses, Passover plate, and lamb patterns. Divide the class into groups and give each a pattern. Have each group color their pattern, glue it to their colored section on the bulletin board, and write about the person or symbol of Passover. Post the pictures and writings to create a visual of the story of Passover.

Reference Verses
Exodus 19-20

Key Bible Verse
It is the LORD your God you must follow, and him you must revere. Keep his commands and obey him; serve him and hold fast to him. Deuteronomy 13:4

Mini-Lesson
In Moses' day, God gave us ten important rules to show us how He wants us to live. By following these rules, we show God that He is important to us, and we are grateful to Him for His guidance.

Materials Needed
Muted-colored butcher paper, Moses with tablets pattern (p. 70), tablet pattern (p. 69), crayons or markers, scissors, light brown paper

Assembly
Cover the bulletin board with muted-colored butcher paper. Enlarge, color, and cut out the Moses with tablets pattern. Post the pattern on the display. Copy ten tablet patterns on light brown paper. Write the simplified commandment text on each pattern (see Sample Text). Cut out the patterns and post them around the display, leaving space beside each one. Have students brainstorm a way to uphold each commandment. Write the students' suggestions beside the corresponding tablet patterns.

Sample Text
1. Trust God only.
2. Worship only God.
3. Use God's name respectfully.
4. Rest and think about God.
5. Respect parents.
6. Protect human life.
7. Be true to your husband or wife.
8. Don't take what belongs to others.
9. Don't lie about others.
10. Don't want what others have.

THE WALLS WILL FALL!

Reference Verses
Joshua 6:1-20

Key Bible Verse
The LORD is my strength and my shield; my heart trusts in him, and I am helped. Psalm 28:7

Mini-Lesson
God won the battle using His strength. The Lord asked Joshua to use his abilities to do the best he could, but ultimately God did the work. When you face something that seems impossible, remember that God will help you through it.

Materials Needed
Light blue butcher paper, Joshua pattern (p. 73), walls of Jericho pattern (p. 71-72), scissors, hook-and-loop fastener, crayons or markers

Assembly
Cover the bulletin board with light blue butcher paper to resemble the sky. Enlarge, color, and cut out the Joshua pattern. Post the pattern on the display. Enlarge and copy two sets of the walls of Jericho pattern. Assemble and attach one set of walls to the display. On the second set of walls, cut out and color the stone shapes. On each set of stones, write a phrase about trusting or counting on God (see Sample Text). Attach a hook-and-loop fastener to the back of each stone and to the corresponding place on the posted wall. Divide the class into small groups and give each a set of stones. Have students "break the secret code" by putting the stones in the correct order to find the hidden messages. Have them attach their messages to the assembled walls on the board. Talk about the importance of trusting God even when things seem impossible.

Sample Text
- Trust in the Lord.
- God will give you strength.
- Always serve God.
- God will help you.
- You can count on God.

Reference Verses
Judges 7

Key Bible Verse
"If you believe, you will receive whatever you ask for in prayer." Matthew 21:22

Mini-Lesson
At first, Gideon did not think his small group of soldiers could defeat a large army, but he did not get discouraged. His belief in God's power helped him win the battle. If you have faith in God and trust His judgement, you can do whatever you need to do. In difficult times, turn to God for strength.

Materials Needed
Muted-colored butcher paper, Gideon and soldier patterns (p. 74), scissors, crayons or markers, trumpet and noise burst patterns (p. 75)

Assembly
Cover the bulletin board with muted-colored butcher paper. Enlarge, color, and cut out the Gideon and soldier patterns. Post the patterns on the board. Have each student cut out and color a trumpet pattern. Then, have students label the patterns with short "trust" words or phrases. Attach the patterns to the board, then give each student a noise burst pattern to write statements about trust and faith in God from the story. Post the completed noise burst patterns at the ends of the trumpet patterns. Encourage students to use key words such as "trust" and "believe" as they write their statements. Allow students to share and explain their writing with the class.

Reference Verses
Ruth 1

Key Bible Verse
Be kind and compassionate to one another, forgiving each other, just as in Christ God forgave you. Ephesians 4:32

Mini-Lesson
Ruth showed her mother-in-law Naomi great kindness by staying with her, even after Ruth's husband died. Doing something nice for someone is how you can show kindness. Comforting a sad friend or helping without being asked are ways to show kindness. What is something else you can do to show love or kindness toward someone?

Materials Needed
light-colored butcher paper, Ruth and Naomi pattern (p. 76), crayons or markers, scissors, joined paper doll pattern (p. 76)

Assembly
Cover the bulletin board with light-colored butcher paper. Enlarge, color, and cut out the Ruth and Naomi pattern. Post the pattern on the board. Give each student a copy of the joined paper doll pattern. Have him decorate one pattern as a self-portrait and the other as a friend. Let students write phrases about friendship and kindness on the banner portion of the patterns. Post the patterns with phrases on the bulletin board. Use the display as a way to remind students about compassion and friendship.

Reference Verses
1 Samuel 3

Key Bible Verse
Blessed is the man who listens to me, watching daily at my doors, waiting at my doorway.
Proverbs 8:34

Mini-Lesson
Samuel answered God's call with respect and obedience. He knew God was mighty and great. Samuel understood that God had a special plan for him. How would you answer if God called on you?

Materials Needed
Dark-colored butcher paper, child in bed pattern (p. 80), crayons or markers, scissors

Assembly
Cover the board with dark-colored butcher paper. Give each student a copy of the child in bed pattern. Have each student decorate her pattern to resemble herself. On the pattern, have her write how she can listen to God. Post the patterns around the board. Talk with students about how God has a special plan for each of them and how important it is for them to read their Bibles often to learn more about how to read the Lord's words.

Reference Verses
1 Samuel 17

Key Bible Verse
"Be strong and courageous. Do not be afraid or terrified because of them, for the Lord your God goes with you; he will never leave you nor forsake you." Deuteronomy 31:6

Mini-Lesson
David knew that muscles and strength were not what he needed to defeat Goliath. He had faith in God and the talents God gave him. Always make the most of the special gifts God has given you. Think about the unique talents God has blessed you with.

Materials Needed
Muted-colored butcher paper, Goliath pattern (p. 77-78), crayons or markers, scissors, David and rock patterns (p. 79)

Assembly
Cover the bulletin board with muted-colored butcher paper. Enlarge, color, and cut out the Goliath pattern. Post him on the display. Copy, color, and cut out the David pattern. Post him on the bulletin board opposite Goliath. Give each student a copy of one of the rock patterns. On the patterns, have students write prayers asking God for strength and bravery. Post the rock patterns between David and Goliath. Ask students to share their prayers and talk about a time when they were scared and asked God for help.

Reference Verses
1 Kings 17

Key Bible Verse
The wild animals honor me, the jackals and the owls, because I provide water in the desert and streams in the wasteland, to give drink to my people, my chosen.... Isaiah 43:20

Mini-Lesson
God provides us with what we need, just as He provided Elijah with food and water to survive. Remember to say prayers of thanks to God for providing you with the things you need each day.

Materials Needed
Bright-colored butcher paper, raven with banner pattern (p. 81), crayons or markers, scissors

Assembly
Cover the bulletin board with bright-colored butcher paper. Give each student a copy of the raven with banner pattern to color and cut out. Have each student use scissors to fringe the edges of the raven's wings. On the banner portion of the patterns, have students write things they are thankful for. Post the completed patterns to the bulletin board. Discuss with students ways they can give back to God for the many daily provisions He gives them.

Josiah became king when he was eight years old.

He was a good king and tried to please God.

He wanted to repair the temple in his kingdom.

During the clean-up, a high preist found the Book of Law.

The priest gave the book to Josiah's secretary.

Josiah learned that his people were not living according to God's word.

Josiah and the Book of the Law

Reference Verses
2 Kings 22-23

Key Bible Verse
"...But you are a forgiving God, gracious and compassionate, slow to anger and abounding in love." Nehemiah 9:17

Mini-Lesson
King Josiah accepted the responsibility of his people's wrongdoing. He took charge and cleaned the temple and his soul! He did God's work with a positive attitude and an open heart. When you are doing chores or something you are responsible for, remember to do the job right with a good attitude.

Materials Needed
Dark-colored butcher paper, King Josiah pattern (p. 86), crayons or markers, scissors, scroll pattern (p. 87), hook-and-loop fasteners

Assembly
Cover the bulletin board with dark-colored butcher paper. Enlarge, color, and cut out the King Josiah pattern. Post the pattern on the board. Enlarge and cut out copies of the scroll pattern. In each pattern, write a portion of the story about King Josiah (see Sample Text). On the bulletin board, draw a matching number of scroll outlines and number them. Attach pieces of hook-and-loop fasteners to the back of each scroll and the matching pieces to the bulletin board. Challenge students by having them correctly order the story of Josiah and the Book of the Law. Talk about how Josiah took responsibility and was forgiven by God.

Sample Text
• Josiah became king when he was eight years old.
• He was as a good king and tried to please God.
• He wanted to repair the temple in his kingdom.
• During the clean-up, a high priest found the Book of the Law
• The priest gave the book to Josiah's secretary.
• Josiah learned that his people were not living according to God's Word.

Reference Verses
Psalm 23

Key Bible Verse
Give thanks to the LORD, for he is good; his love endures forever. Psalm 107:1

Mini-Lesson
A shepherd makes sure his sheep have food, water, and shelter. He also protects the sheep from predators and thieves. God is our shepherd, watching over us and giving us what we need. Remember to thank God each day for taking care of you.

Materials Needed
Green butcher paper, shepherd pattern (p. 83), crayons or markers, scissors, sentence strips, hook-and-loop fasteners, lamb pattern (p. 68), elbow-shaped pasta painted white, glue

Assembly
Cover the bulletin board with green butcher paper to indicate a pasture. Enlarge, color, and cut out the shepherd pattern. Post the pattern on the display. Use sentence strips to write each of the verses from the Shepherd's Psalm (if desired). Attach a hook-and-loop fastener to the back of each sentence strip and to its match on the bulletin board. Attach the sentences to the display. Give each student a copy of the lamb pattern. Have her color and cut out the pattern, then decorate it using white, painted elbow-shaped pasta and glue. Accent the display using the completed lamb patterns. Use this bulletin board as a tool to help students learn the prayer. Begin by posting one verse at a time, explaining its meaning. After students are familiar with the prayer, allow them to put the verses in the correct order.

Reference Verses
Proverbs 3:5-6, 6:6-11, 12:16, 17:9, and 20:22

Key Bible Verse
Surely you desire truth in the inner parts; you teach me wisdom in the inmost place. Psalm 51:6

Mini-Lesson
There is wisdom in God's Word. The book of Proverbs is full of many wonderful truths that tell us how to avoid trouble and find truth. Learn from God's wise words and use His teachings to make good choices.

Materials Needed
Green butcher paper, brown butcher paper, owl and speech bubble patterns (p. 82), scissors, crayons or markers

Assembly
Cover the bulletin board with green butcher paper to indicate green leaves. Cut a large top border from brown butcher paper. Post it at the top of the display. Enlarge, color, and cut out five copies of the owl pattern. Enlarge and cut out five copies of the speech bubble pattern. Divide the class into small groups. Assign each group one of the Reference Verses to read. Have each group write what the verse means in the speech bubble. Display the owls with the appropriate speech bubbles. Have each group explain how students can incorporate the teachings into their lives.

Reference Verses
Isaiah 9:6-7

Key Bible Verse
"Blessed are the peacemakers, for they will be called sons of God." Matthew 5:9

Mini-Lesson
In the Old Testament, God's people were told about Jesus the Savior. He was referred to by many names but one that was especially important was Prince of Peace. While on the earth, Jesus taught people about peace and kindness. God wants all of us to work toward peace. How can you be a peacemaker?

Materials Needed
White, red, orange, yellow, green, blue, and purple butcher paper, dove pattern (p. 84), scissors, paper strips

Assembly
Cover the bulletin board with white butcher paper. Cut rounded strips of red, orange, yellow, green, blue, and purple butcher paper and post them on the board to resemble a rainbow. Give each student a copy of the dove pattern to cut out. Provide students with thin white paper strips and have them write how they can show compassion and be peacemakers. Post the doves on the rainbow beside the students' writing. Use this display as a positive reminder to students of how they can promote peace and kindness daily.

Reference Verses
Isaiah 40:1-5

Key Bible Verse
Praise be to the God and Father of our Lord Jesus Christ, the Father of compassion and the God of all comfort. 2 Corinthians 1:3

Mini-Lesson
In this passage in Isaiah, we are told about how God proclaimed comfort for His people. Today, God is here to offer comfort to us. Don't be afraid to share your feelings with God. Can you think of a time when you asked God to help you feel less afraid or sad?

Materials Needed
White butcher paper, teddy bear pattern (p. 84), six quilt square patterns (p. 85), crayons or markers, scissors, black marker

Assembly
Cover the bulletin board with white butcher paper. Give each student a copy of the teddy bear pattern and a quilt square pattern to decorate and cut out. Let students decorate the quilt square and bear patterns. Then, have each student write a phrase of comfort about God on the quilt square. After coloring the teddy bear pattern, have each student label it with his name. Post the quilt squares in the middle of the board, leaving a small space between them. Next to the completed class quilt, post the teddy bear patterns. Accent the display by drawing "stitch marks" between the squares using a black marker. Explain how God comforts us, just as a reassuring teddy bear or a soft, warm quilt.

Reference Verses
Daniel 5

Key Bible Verse
"You shall have no other gods before me."
Exodus 20:3

Mini-Lesson
Through Daniel, God showed His power and strength to King Belshazzar. He showed him that He is the only God and is stronger than anyone or anything. God not only expects us to worship and trust in Him only, He commands it. If you trust in God, He will be with you.

Materials Needed
Dark-colored butcher paper, Daniel pattern (p. 88), crayons or markers, scissors, wall patterns (p. 88-89), laminate or clear contact paper, secret code pattern (p. 90), glue, write on/wipe off markers

Assembly
Cover the board with dark-colored butcher paper. Enlarge, color, and cut out the Daniel pattern. Post the pattern on the display. Enlarge and cut out each wall pattern. Laminate the wall patterns or cover them with clear contact paper. Post them on the bulletin board. Copy and cut out the secret code pattern and glue it on a smaller wall pattern. Post it at the bottom of the display. Challenge students to use the secret code to decipher the hidden message on each wall (see Sample Text). Let them write the messages beneath the code symbols using a write on/wipe off marker.

Sample Text
• Worship only God.
• All you need is God.
• God is awesome.
• God is always with you.
• God's way is the only way.
• Have faith in God.

Reference Verses
Daniel 6

Key Bible Verse
Is any one of you in trouble? He should pray. Is anyone happy? Let him sing songs of praise.
James 5:13

Mini-Lesson
Daniel showed courage by doing what was right even when others disagreed. He was not even afraid to stand up all by himself, for God had given him courage. Courage means saying or doing what you believe, even when it is difficult. Can you think of a time when you were courageous?

Materials Needed
Dark-colored butcher paper, Daniel and the lions pattern (p. 92), crayons or markers, scissors, lion pattern (p. 91), spiral-shaped pasta painted yellow and orange, glue

Assembly
Cover the bulletin board with dark-colored butcher paper. Enlarge, color, and cut out the Daniel and the lions pattern. Post the pattern on the board. Give each student a copy of the lion pattern to color and cut out. Have students glue pieces of spiral-shaped pasta painted yellow and orange to the lions' manes on the patterns. After the patterns have dried, have students write prayers asking for courage and guidance on the patterns (if desired). Post the patterns around the bulletin board. Talk about how God gave Daniel courage and how He can give us courage also.

Reference Verses
Jonah 1-4

Key Bible Verse
"...In my distress I called to the Lord, and he answered me. From the depths of the grave I called for help, and you listened to my cry." Jonah 2:2

Mini-Lesson
God asked Jonah to do something that he really didn't want to do. God helped Jonah to obey His Word. When you have disobeyed God, tell Him you are sorry and ask Him to guide you to do what is right.

Materials Needed
Blue butcher paper, Jonah in the whale pattern (p. 93-94), crayons or markers, scissors, whale pattern (p. 95), blue plastic wrap or cellophane paper

Assembly
Cover the bulletin board with blue butcher paper to resemble water. Enlarge, copy, and color the Jonah in the whale pattern. Post the pattern on the display. Give each student a copy of the whale pattern to color and cut out. Inside the pattern, have students write the lessons that they learned from the story of Jonah and the whale. Post the whales on the display. Create an underwater effect on the bulletin board by attaching lengths of blue plastic wrap or cellophane paper. Refer to the display to help students remember key lessons from the story.

Reference Verses
Luke 2:8-20

Key Bible Verse
Come, let us bow down in worship, let us kneel before the LORD our Maker. Psalm 95:6

Mini-Lesson
We all enjoy giving and receiving gifts. God gave us a special gift—His son Jesus. That is why we celebrate Christmas—to recognize the birth of our Savior. Be sure to take this wonderful gift from God and accept Jesus into your life.

Materials Needed
Dark blue butcher paper, Mary, Joseph, and baby Jesus pattern (p. 109), baby Jesus pattern (p. 110), crayons or markers, scissors, glue, yellow chenille craft sticks or Spanish moss, construction paper

Assembly
Cover the bulletin board with dark blue butcher paper. Enlarge, color, and cut out the Mary, Joseph, and baby Jesus pattern. Post the pattern on the display. Give each student a copy of the baby Jesus pattern to color and cut out. Have students glue yellow chenille craft sticks or Spanish moss to the pattern to resemble hay. Provide construction paper for each student to make a birthday card for baby Jesus. Encourage students to write a special birthday message for baby Jesus inside the card (if desired). Post the completed cards under each student's pattern. Talk about how the true meaning of Christmas is to celebrate the birth of Jesus and His love for us.

A Wonderful Journey

Reference Verses
Matthew 2:1-12

Key Bible Verse
For great is his love toward us, and the faithfulness of the LORD endures forever. Psalm 117:2

Mini-Lesson
The Magi traveled a long way to see Jesus. Even when King Herod tried to trick them, they were faithful to their mission. When the Magi arrived at Jesus' home they bowed down and worshipped the child. God helped the wise men by sending a star to guide them. Think of a time when you felt discouraged or were unsure of the way you should go. Did you ask God for help?

Materials Needed
Dark blue butcher paper, light blue butcher paper, Magi pattern (p. 96), crayons or markers, scissors, young Jesus pattern (p. 97), star patterns (p. 98), star in window pattern (p. 97), poster board, laminate or clear contact paper, hook-and-loop fasteners

Assembly
Cover the bulletin board with dark blue butcher paper to resemble the night sky. Post a winding strip of light blue butcher paper to make a path. Enlarge, color, and cut out the Magi pattern. Post the pattern in the top left corner of the display. Enlarge, color, and cut out the young Jesus pattern and the star in window pattern. Post the patterns in the bottom right corner. Enlarge, copy, and cut out five star patterns. Post them along the winding path. In some of the star patterns, write a key event from the story on each pattern (see Sample Text). Mount each one on poster board and laminate or cover with clear contact paper. Attach the matching pieces of hook-and-loop fasteners to the back of each star pattern and to the posted star patterns. Challenge students to arrange the story in the correct order.

Sample Text
• Herod hears that a king will be born in Bethlehem.
• Herod asks the Magi to tell him where the baby is.
• The Magi are guided by a great star.
• The Magi worship Jesus.
• God warns the Magi to travel home another way.

FISHERS OF MEN

Reference Verses
Luke 5:1-11

Key Bible Verse
"Come, follow me," Jesus said, "and I will make you fishers of men." Matthew 4:19

Mini-Lesson
Jesus chose twelve disciples. They learned from Jesus and helped spread His Word. Make a promise to follow the words and examples of Jesus in your life.

Materials Needed
Dark blue butcher paper, light blue butcher paper, crayons or markers, scissors, two brown grocery bags, children patterns (p. 117), fish pattern (p. 112), yarn

Assembly
Cover the bottom half of the bulletin board with dark blue butcher paper to resemble water. Cover the top half of the board with light blue butcher paper to resemble the sky. Draw and cut out a large boat shape from two brown grocery bags and attach it to the center of the display. Make several copies of the children patterns and write a specific situation on each one (if desired). Post the patterns in the boat. Make several copies of the fish pattern and give one to each student. Have students write solutions to the situations shown on the fish (if desired). Attach each fish to the matching child pattern using lengths of yarn. Accent the display posting extra fish patterns along the bottom of the bulletin board.

Share Your Christian Attitude; Follow the Beatitudes

Reference Verses
Matthew 5:1-16

Key Bible Verse
"Now then, my sons, listen to me; blessed are those who keep my ways. Listen to my instruction and be wise; do not ignore it." Proverbs 8:32-33

Mini-Lesson
God blesses those who follow Jesus. Jesus' followers strive to be peaceful and gentle, just as Jesus was when He was on Earth. One way to serve God is to act peacefully towards others and to have a kind attitude. Think about some ways you can show peace and kindness to others.

Materials Needed
Muted-colored butcher paper, banner pattern (p. 105), crayons or markers, scissors

Assembly
Cover the bulletin board with muted-colored butcher paper. Divide the class into small groups. Assign each group a verse from the Beatitudes (Matthew 5:3-12) and give each group a copy of the banner pattern to color and cut out. Let each group paraphrase their assigned verse, then write it on the banner. Post the banners on the board and have students share the meaning of their verse with the class.

Reference Verses
Matthew 6:5-15

Key Bible Verse
But you, dear friends, build yourselves up in your most holy faith and pray in the Holy Spirit.
Jude 1:20

Mini-Lesson
How should you talk to God? You can talk directly to God just as you would your mom or dad or a friend. In the book of Matthew we are given a good example of how to pray. In your prayers, remember to thank God for your blessings, ask for His forgiveness of sins, and ask Him for help with a problem or concern. Remember to talk to God by praying every day.

Materials Needed
Dark-colored butcher paper, Jesus pattern (p. 99-100), crayons or markers, scissors, yellow construction paper, praying child pattern (p. 102)

Assembly
Cover the bulletin board with dark-colored butcher paper. Enlarge, color, and cut out the Jesus pattern. On the robe portion of the Jesus pattern, write the Lord's Prayer (see Sample Text). Post the pattern in the center of the display. Highlight the Jesus pattern with yellow construction paper cut to resemble a holy glow. Give each student a copy of the praying child pattern to color and label with his name (if desired). Recite the Lord's Prayer with the class and encourage them to memorize it. As each student is able to recite the prayer, post his child praying pattern on the bulletin board.

Sample Text
Our Father which art in heaven, Hallowed be thy name. Thy kingdom come, Thy will be done in earth, as it is in heaven. Give us this day our daily bread. And forgive us our debts, as we forgive our debtors. And lead us not into temptation, but deliver us from evil: For thine is the kingdom, and the power, and the glory, for ever. Amen.

Reference Verses
Matthew 7:1-12

Key Bible Verse
And the Lord's servant must not quarrel; instead, he must be kind to everyone, able to teach, not resentful. 2 Timothy 2:24

Mini-Lesson
God wants us to treat others kindly, as we would like to be treated. This means saying and doing things to make other people feel happier or better about themselves. Remember when you are dealing with other people to think about how would you like to be treated.

Materials Needed
Dark-colored butcher paper, bag of gold pattern (p. 103), crayons or markers, scissors, yellow construction paper, gold coin pattern (p. 103), glue, gold glitter

Assembly
Cover the bulletin board with dark-colored butcher paper. Enlarge, color, and cut out the bag of gold pattern. Write the "Golden Rule" verse (Matthew 7:12) on the pattern. Post the pattern in the middle of the board. Highlight the bag of gold pattern with yellow construction paper cut with jagged edges to give it a shiny effect. Give each student a copy of the gold coin pattern. Have students write things they can do to live by the "Golden Rule" on the patterns. Let students put a ring of glue around the edges of their patterns, then cover the glue with gold glitter. Post the coin patterns around the bag of gold. Accent the title of the display by tracing the letters in gold glitter. Have students share their thoughts about living by the "Golden Rule" and why God wants us to follow it.

Reference Verses
John 4:1-42

Key Bible Verse
...Jesus stood and said in a loud voice, "If anyone is thirsty, let him come to me and drink." John 7:37

Mini-Lesson
The woman at the well had led a sinful life, yet Jesus offered her forgiveness. Jesus offered her living water, which means eternal life. The woman believed in Jesus and told many others about Him. In what ways can you show others about Jesus' love for them?

Materials Needed
Muted-colored butcher paper, woman pattern (p. 120), well pattern (p. 121), crayons or markers, scissors, water drop pattern (p. 120)

Assembly
Cover the bulletin board with muted-colored butcher paper. Enlarge, color, and cut out the woman and well patterns. Post them in the center of the display. Across the top of the well, paraphrase or write the verse John 4:14, "Whoever drinks the water I give him will never thirst." Give each student a copy of the water drop pattern to cut out. Have students write short phrase about God's love for us on the patterns. Place the water drop patterns on the display around the well. Talk with students about how God loves us and how they can share His love with others.

Reference Verses
Luke 8:1-15

Key Bible Verse
"But your hearts must be fully committed to the LORD our God, to live by his decrees and obey his commands, as at this time." 1 Kings 8:61

Mini-Lesson
Read and follow God's Word like a healthy plant soaks up water and sunshine. As you read through the Bible, think about God's teachings and strive to obey them. Remember that God's Word will help you grow into a healthy young person when you open your heart and listen to Him.

Materials Needed
Blue butcher paper, green butcher paper, flower pattern (p. 111), crayons or markers, scissors, seed packet pattern (p. 110), yellow construction paper

Assembly
Cover the top half of the bulletin board with blue butcher paper to resemble the sky. Cover the bottom half of the pattern with green butcher paper to resemble grass. Give each student a copy of the flower pattern to cut out and color. Have students write how they can "soak up" God's Word on the stems of their flowers (if desired). Post the flowers on the display to create a garden. Accent the bulletin board by posting an enlarged copy of the seed packet pattern, along with a sun cut from yellow construction paper. Write positive Godly growth messages on the seed packet pattern (see Sample Text). Use the instructions on the seed packet to teach the class how they can learn from God's Word.

Sample Text
- Open your heart.
- Soak up God's Word daily.
- Soon your faith will grow strong.

Reference Verses
John 6:1-14

Key Bible Verse
Give thanks to the Lord, for he is good; his love endures forever. Psalm 107:1

Mini-Lesson
While on Earth, Jesus showed how much He cared for the people around Him, and in the story of the loaves and fish He showed it by providing the crowd with food when they were hungry. Think of something you can do for some of the people in your life to show much you care about them.

Materials Needed
Muted-colored butcher paper, paper tablecloth, crayons or markers, file folders, fish and loaf patterns (p. 112), scissors, glue, hook-and-loop fasteners

Assembly
Cover the bulletin board with muted-colored butcher paper. Attach a large paper tablecloth to the center of the display. Have students draw self-portraits around the edges of the tablecloth so they look as if they are sitting at the table. Give each student a file folder, several fish and loaf patterns to cut out and color. Have each student glue two fish and five loaf patterns on the outside of her file folder. Then, have her open the folder and glue many fish and loaf patterns inside to show how Jesus made the food multiply. Post the folders on the board and attach a piece of hook-and-loop fastener to the top of each one so it can be opened as you review the story. Allow students to write messages about God's bounty and compassion on the tablecloth (if desired). Accent the display with extra copies of the fish pattern along the top and bottom of the bulletin board.

Reference Verses
John 6:25-58

Key Bible Verse
And my God will meet all your needs according to his glorious riches in Christ Jesus. Philippians 4:19

Mini-Lesson
God meets your everyday needs, whether it be food or strength or faith. In this passage, Jesus explained He can also meet your most important need, and it is "the bread of life." He meant that through Him you can have your most important need met through Him—salvation. He is food for your soul. By living your life as Jesus did, you are "feeding" your soul daily. It's important to eat the bread of life often. Read the Bible and pray each day to be a strong Christian.

Materials Needed
Dark-colored butcher paper, grocery bag pattern (p. 118), scissors, bread pattern (p. 112), apple, pear, carrot patterns (p. 118), grapes, grapefruit patterns (p. 122), banana, pineapple, lemon, orange, strawberry patterns (p. 125), crayons or markers, glue

Assembly
Cover the bulletin board with dark-colored butcher paper. Give each student a copy of the grocery bag pattern to cut out. Have each student personalize the top of his bag with his own store name. Provide copies of the various food patterns for students to color and cut out. Have them glue the food patterns inside their bags. On the writing space on each bag, have students write the name of their favorite Bible story or verse that "feeds their soul." Post the bags and encourage students to refer to the display for their daily bread.

Reference Verses
Luke 10:25-37

Key Bible Verse
Therefore, as God's chosen people, holy and dearly loved, clothe yourselves with compassion, kindness, humility, gentleness and patience. Colossians 3:12

Mini-Lesson
In the story of the Good Samaritan, a stranger shows great compassion for someone he didn't even know. Compassion means that you understand another person's needs and are willing to help, even if it is hard work. It means doing what you can to help someone when they need it. Think of ways you can show compassion toward someone.

Materials Needed
Bright-colored butcher paper, paper doll pattern (p. 107), crayons or markers, scissors, construction paper

Assembly
Cover the bulletin board with bright-colored butcher paper. Give each student a copy of the paper doll pattern to decorate and cut out. Then, have each student trace their hands onto construction paper and cut out two handprints. On their handprint patterns, have each student write a statement about how he can show compassion (if desired). Post the completed patterns along the left and right sides of the bulletin board. Accent the display's title by making a few enlarged self-made handprint patterns using construction paper and posting them in small clusters on each side of the title. Allow each student to share how he plans to show compassion to others.

Reference Verses
Luke 10:38-42

Key Bible Verse
"My sheep listen to my voice; I know them, and they follow me." John 10:27

Mini-Lesson
God wants us to listen to His Word and do our best to obey Him. God has a plan for each person, and by learning about the things Jesus said and did, you can learn His plan for you. As Jesus told Martha, it is most important to listen to Him. Make a promise to read about Jesus and live by His teachings each day.

Materials Needed
Muted-colored butcher paper, telephone and receiver patterns (p. 106), crayons or markers, scissors, black marker, index cards

Assembly
Cover the bulletin board with muted-colored butcher paper. Give each student a copy of the telephone and receiver patterns. Have them color and cut out the patterns. Post the matching telephone and receiver patterns beside each other. Connect the matching patterns by drawing a coil line using a black marker. Provide index cards for students to write important things God wants them to hear and remember. Post the messages beside the appropriate telephones. Share with students that reading the Bible daily will help them hear God's instructions.

Reference Verses
Luke 15:11-32

Key Bible Verse
"I will be a Father to you, and you will be my sons and daughters, says the Lord Almighty." 2 Corinthians 6:18

Mini-Lesson
The father in the story loved his son, no matter how foolish or irresponsibly he had behaved. God treats us the same way. He is our kind and loving Heavenly Father. When we, His children, make mistakes, we can ask for and receive His forgiveness.

Materials Needed
Bright-colored butcher paper, house pattern (p. 114-115), crayons or markers, scissors, father pattern (p. 113), son pattern (p. 112), paper squares, construction paper, stapler, hook-and-loop fasteners

Assembly
Cover the bulletin board with bright-colored butcher paper. Enlarge, color, and cut out the house pattern. Post it on the board. Enlarge, color, and cut out the father and son patterns. Post the son on the left side of display and the father near the doorway of the house. Then, provide paper squares for students to write welcoming or forgiving phrases. Have students share their phrases. Staple the phrases over the windows of the house. Place small flaps of construction paper over each message. Attach a hook-and-loop fastener on the back of each paper flap so that students can open each window to reveal the father's loving messages.

Reference Verses
Mark 10:13-16

Key Bible Verse
Jesus said, "Let the little children come to me, and do not hinder them, for the kingdom of heaven belongs to such as these." Matthew 19:14

Mini-Lesson
Jesus loves everyone, especially children. In the New Testament, He often referred to how special children are. Children can know and trust God just as grown-ups can. Jesus knows how unique you are. What special gifts did God give you?

Materials Needed
Dark-colored butcher paper, Jesus pattern (p. 99-101), crayons or markers, scissors, heart patterns (p. 108), paper doll pattern (p. 107)

Assembly
Cover the bulletin board with dark-colored butcher paper. Enlarge, color, and cut out the Jesus pattern. Post the pattern at the top of the display. Enlarge and cut out three large heart patterns and post them in the background. Give each student a paper doll pattern and a small heart pattern. Have students decorate the paper doll patterns. Let them write their names on the heart patterns (if desired). Attach the patterns to the bulletin board in a circle to create a wreath. Write the phrase "Jesus Loves the Little Children" in the center of the wreath. Enlarge and cut out two copies of the small heart pattern. Write the chapter and verse of the Reference and Key Bible Verses on each pattern and use them to accent the display. Add a few small hearts to complete the bulletin board. Talk with students about times they felt loved by God.

Reference Verses
Luke 19:1-10

Key Bible Verse
Search in me, O God, and know my heart; test me and know my anxious thoughts. Psalm 139:23

Mini-Lesson
Zaccheus was a tax collector who had cheated many people of their money. When he heard Jesus, he realized that he had been wrong. He had what is called "a change of heart," which means he turned from his old ways and acted differently. God loves us even when we make mistakes or act unkindly. If we try to change our ways, God will forgive us. We all can improve something about ourselves. Think of what you can do to be a better person and show God's love.

Materials Needed
Blue butcher paper, heart patterns (p. 108), crayons or markers, scissors, glue

Assembly
Cover the bulletin board with blue butcher paper. Accent the bulletin board background by posting two enlarged colored copies of the large heart pattern. Give each student a copy of the large and small heart patterns to color and cut out. On the smaller heart pattern, have each student write something she can do to be a better Christian. Then, have each student glue the small heart in the center of the large heart. Post the patterns on the bulletin board. Allow each student to share how she is going to strive to be a better Christian. Accent the bottom with a border made from small heart patterns.

Reference Verses
John 12

Key Bible Verse
Therefore I will praise you among the nations, O Lord; I will sing praises to your name. Psalm 18:49

Mini-Lesson
Just before Jesus was crucified, He was greeted and worshipped as He entered Jerusalem. Today we still honor Him by worshipping and praising Him. Praising God helps you feel closer to Him. When and how do you praise God?

Materials Needed
Muted-color butcher paper, Jesus riding the donkey pattern (p. 119), crayons or markers, scissors, palm leaf pattern (p. 119), green paper

Assembly
Cover the bulletin board with muted-colored butcher paper. Enlarge, color, and cut out the Jesus riding the donkey pattern. Post it in the center of the display. Make several copies of the palm leaf pattern copied onto green paper. Give each student a copy of the palm leaf pattern to cut out. Let each student use scissors to cut lines into her pattern to create leaf edges. Attach the patterns to the display along the bottom and top of the board. Enlarge several copies of the palm leaf pattern for students to color and then write phrases praising Jesus (if desired). Find out from students how they feel after praising Jesus.

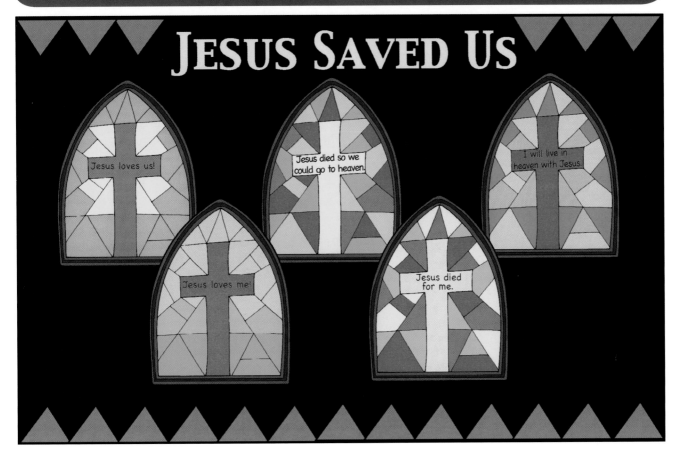

Reference Verses
Matthew 27:32-56

Key Bible Verse
The Lord is not slow in keeping his promise, as some understand slowness. He is patient with you, not wanting anyone to perish, but everyone to come to repentance. 2 Peter 3:9

Mini-Lesson
When you want to know God and ask forgiveness for your sins, God will forgive you. When you are truly sorry in your heart and work to change your ways, God will help you. Jesus died for everyone's sins so that each of us could live in heaven. We just need to accept Him into our hearts.

Materials Needed
Black butcher paper, stained glass pattern (p. 104), crayons or markers, scissors

Assembly
Cover the bulletin board with black butcher paper. Give each student a copy of the stained glass pattern. Have each student cut out the pattern and color it. On the cross, have students write about Jesus and His love for us. Post the completed patterns on the bulletin board. Use the display to talk about how God loved us so much that He gave us His only Son to take away our sins and give us peace in heaven.

Reference Verses
Luke 24

Key Bible Verse
For what I received I passed on to you as of first importance: that Christ died for our sins according to the Scriptures. Corinthians 15:3

Mini-Lesson
Jesus died in a very painful way. But because He died, we are able to know God and live in His kingdom forever. Sometimes something good can come from something sad or painful. Know that no matter what the situation is, God has given us the gift of salvation. So no matter how difficult a situation may seem, you can have hope through Christ.

Materials Needed
Brown butcher paper, Jesus outside the tomb pattern (p. 116), crayons or markers, scissors, draped cross pattern (p. 116)

Assembly
Cover the bulletin board with brown butcher paper. Enlarge, color, and cut out the Jesus outside the tomb pattern. Post it on the left side of the board. Give each student a copy of the draped cross pattern to color and cut out. On each pattern, have students tell how Jesus' ascension to heaven gives us hope and eternal life (if desired). Post the patterns around the display and let students share their thoughts with the class.

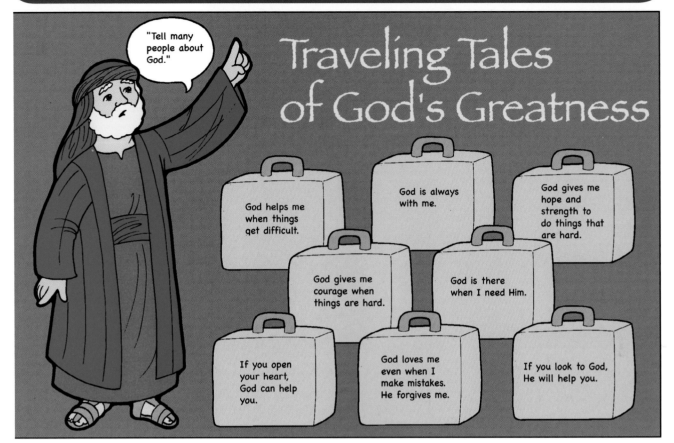

Reference Verses
Acts 9

Key Bible Verse
Therefore, if anyone is in Christ, he is a new creation; the old has gone, the new has come!
2 Corinthians 5:17

Mini-Lesson
Saul was known to arrest and hurt Christians. One day, while he was traveling towards Damascus, the Lord came to Saul and changed his heart. After that, Saul became committed to telling people about God. What can you tell others about God?

Materials Needed
Bright-colored butcher paper, Saul pattern (p. 122), crayons or markers, scissors, speech balloon pattern (p. 82), suitcase pattern (p. 123)

Assembly
Cover the bulletin board with bright-colored butcher paper. Enlarge, color, and cut out the Saul pattern. Copy and cut out the speech balloon pattern. Inside the speech balloon write "Tell many people about God." Attach it to the display beside the pattern of Saul. Give each student a copy of the suitcase pattern to color and cut out. On the pattern, have each student write about the importance of God in his life and how God helps people. Post the suitcase patterns on the display. Then, encourage students to talk about the importance of sharing their stories of God's love.

Reference Verses
Romans 12:3-8

Key Bible Verse
For it is by grace you have been saved, through faith—and this is not from yourselves, it is the gift of God. Ephesians 2:8

Mini-Lesson
God has given each of us special gifts. You can know that you are a special and unique person that God has made. It is important for you to use your gifts, whatever they are by teaching others or serving them, you should practice your God-given gifts.

Materials Needed
Light-colored butcher paper, gift pattern (p. 121), crayons or markers, scissors, paper strips, paper, stapler

Assembly
Cover the bulletin board with light-colored butcher paper. Divide the class into small groups. Assign each group one of the gifts—prophecy, service, teaching, encouragement, giving, leadership, and mercy. Provide each group a copy of the gift pattern to decorate and cut out. Attach a piece of paper, decorated similarly to the gift wrap, to the edge of the bow. Have students write their assigned gift on the bow strip. Give each group a paper strip (approximately the length of the gift pattern) to write the definition for their assigned gift. Staple the definitions on top of the coordinating gift patterns and post them on the display. Instruct students to lift the paper up to reveal the gift definitions underneath. As the class discusses their gifts, remind students that we have all been given one extra special gift—God's love.

Reference Verses
Galatians 5:22-25

Key Bible Verse
May integrity and uprightness protect me, because my hope is in you. Psalm 25:21

Mini-Lesson
We should try to live our lives like Jesus did. The Fruit of the Spirit is love, joy, peace, patience, kindness, goodness, faithfulness, gentleness, and self-control. These are all traits that Jesus had. By incorporating these things into our lives, we can have His spirit in our hearts. Ask God to help you be more like Jesus and display these traits.

Materials Needed
Blue butcher paper, tree pattern (p. 125-126), crayons or markers, scissors, apple and pear patterns (p. 118), grapes and grapefruit patterns (p. 122), orange, banana, pineapple, lemon, and strawberry patterns (p.125), hook-and loop fasteners, nine poster boards

Assembly
Cover the bulletin board with blue butcher paper. Enlarge, color, and cut out the tree pattern. Post the tree on the bulletin board. Color and cut out all nine of the fruit patterns and label each with one of the Spirit traits. Attach a piece of hook-and-loop fastener to the back of each fruit pattern and its matching piece in the tree leaves. Post the fruits on the tree. Using nine poster boards, write a clue for each fruit and post them around the tree (see Sample Text). Attach a piece of hook-and-loop fastener to the end of each poster. Have students read the clues to match the correct fruit.

Sample Text
- Causes other fruit to be productive (love)
- It helps you put God first (self-control)
- People can depend on you (faithfulness)
- You'll always be ready to help others (kindness)
- Helps you not give up (patience)
- Gives you power not to be rude (gentleness)
- Protects your heart and mind (peace)
- Overcomes any evil (goodness)
- Offers you supernatural strength (joy)

Reference Verses
Ephesians 6:10-20

Key Bible Verse
"So do not fear, for I am with you; do not be dismayed, for I am your God." Isaiah 41:10

Mini-Lesson
Making the right choices can be hard, especially when it seems that everyone else is doing the wrong thing. With God's power, you can stand up against evil and do what's right. He has given you special protection. So put on the armor of God, and you will be able to stand strong.

Materials Needed
Purple butcher paper, soldier pattern (p. 127), crayons or markers, scissors

Assembly
Cover the bulletin board with purple butcher paper. Enlarge a copy of the soldier pattern to give to each student. Talk with students about the armor of God and what each piece represents. Explain the belt of truth, breastplate of righteousness, feet fitted with the gospel of peace, shield of faith, helmet of salvation, and the sword of the Spirit. Have students color and label each piece of the armor on the patterns (if desired). Have students cut out the the face portion of their patterns and draw self-portraits of their faces. Post the patterns on the display to create an "army of God." Add a smaller copy of the soldier pattern with each of the pieces of armor labeled for student reference. Explain to students how they can use the armor of God in their everyday lives.

Reference Verses
Phillippians 2

Key Bible Verse
The fear of the LORD teaches a man wisdom, and humility comes before honor.
Proverbs 15:33

Mini-Lesson
Jesus came into the world to do what God wanted Him to do. He did not want attention or special privledges, for He was humble. Being humble means putting others before yourself and helping them even when you do not get recognition. How can you be like Jesus?

Materials Needed
Blue butcher paper, Jesus pattern (p. 99-101), crayons or markers, scissors, heaven and footstep patterns (p. 128)

Assembly
Cover the bulletin board with blue butcher paper. Enlarge, color, and cut out the Jesus pattern. Post the pattern on the left side of the display. Enlarge, color, and cut out the heaven pattern. Post the pattern on the right side of the display. Enlarge and cut out a footstep pattern for each student. Have students write about how they can be humble servants of God on their patterns (if desired). Post the completed footstep patterns to create a path from Jesus to heaven. Explain to students that as Christians we should follow in Jesus' footsteps and strive to live our lives as He lived His.

Reference Verses
Revelation 21:1-22:6

Key Bible Verse
"Blessed is the king who comes in the name of the Lord! Peace in heaven and glory in the highest!" Luke 19:38

Mini-Lesson
The apostle John saw visions of what heaven would be like. He wrote that heaven is a beautiful place where there is no sadness or tears. If you believe in Jesus the Savior, it is where you will live with God forever. What do you imagine heaven will look like?

Materials Needed
Light blue butcher paper, John pattern (p. 124), crayons or markers, scissors, white drawing paper, white material batting

Assembly
Cover the bulletin board with light blue butcher paper. Enlarge, color, and cut out the John pattern. Post the pattern on the board. Give each student a large sheet of white drawing paper. Read Revelation 21:1-22:6 aloud to the class and have students talk about the things mentioned about heaven. Then, let each student illustrate what she thinks heaven will look like based on the Bible verses. Post the illustrations on the bulletin board under the title "Visions of Heaven." Accent the display with a white cloud using white material batting cut into a large cloud shape.

Use with the *Creation* bulletin board, page 5.

Use with the *Creation* bulletin board, page 5.

 CD-204003 *Interactive Bible Story Bulletin Boards*

Use with the *Creation* bulletin board, page 5.

Use with the *Adam and Eve* bulletin board, page 6.

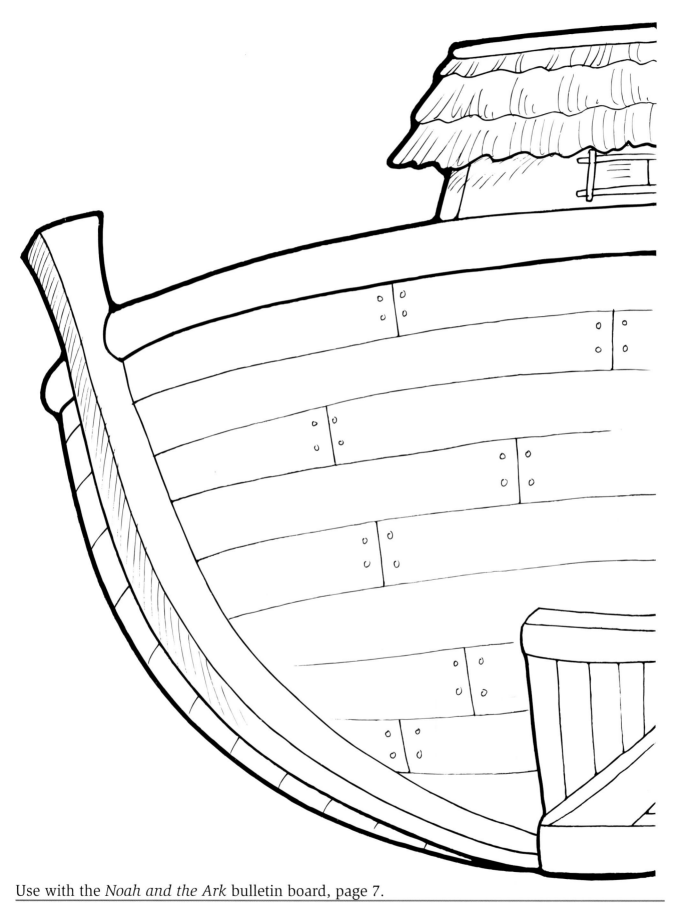

Use with the *Noah and the Ark* bulletin board, page 7.

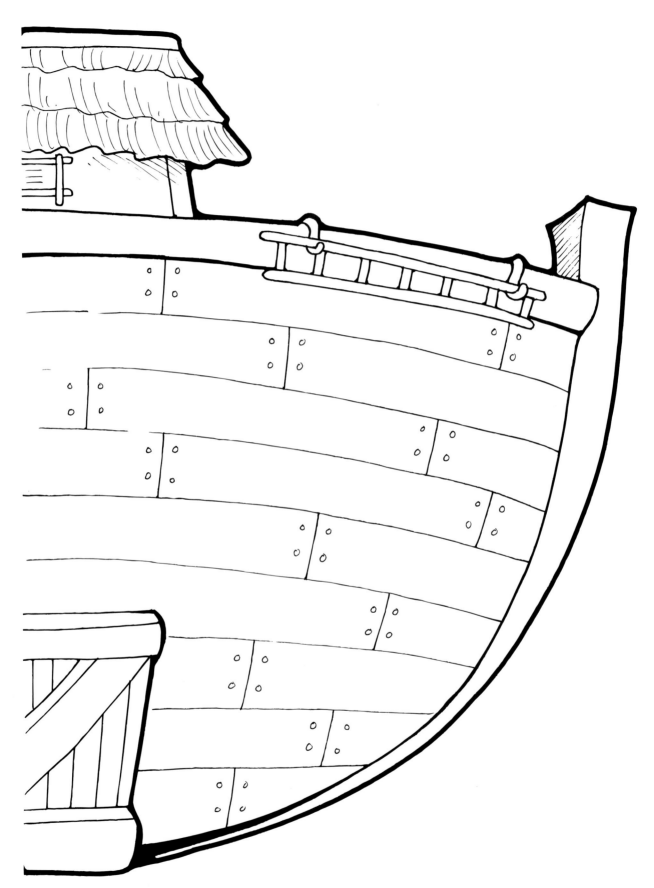

Use with the *Noah and the Ark* bulletin board, page 7.

Use with the *Noah and the Ark* and *God's Promises to Abraham* bulletin boards, pages 7-8.

Use with the *God's Promise to Abraham* bulletin board, page 8.

Use with the *Joseph and the Colorful Coat* bulletin board, page 9.

Use with the *Joseph and the Colorful Coat* bulletin board, page 9.

Use with the *Moses in the River* and *Moses and the Burning Bush* bulletin boards, pages 10-11.

 CD-204003 *Interactive Bible Story Bulletin Boards*

Use with the *Moses in the River* and *Moses and the Burning Bush* bulletin boards, pages 10-11.

 CD-204003 *Interactive Bible Story Bulletin Boards*

Use with the *Moses and the Burning Bush*, *The Ten Plagues of Egypt*, and *Passover* bulletin boards, pages 11-13.

Use with *The Ten Plagues of Egypt* and *Passover* bulletin boards, pages 12-13.

Use with *The Ten Plagues of Egypt* bulletin board, page 12.

Use with *The Ten Plagues of Egypt, Passover,* and *The Shepherd Psalm* bulletin boards, pages 12-13, 22.

CD-204003 *Interactive Bible Story Bulletin Boards*

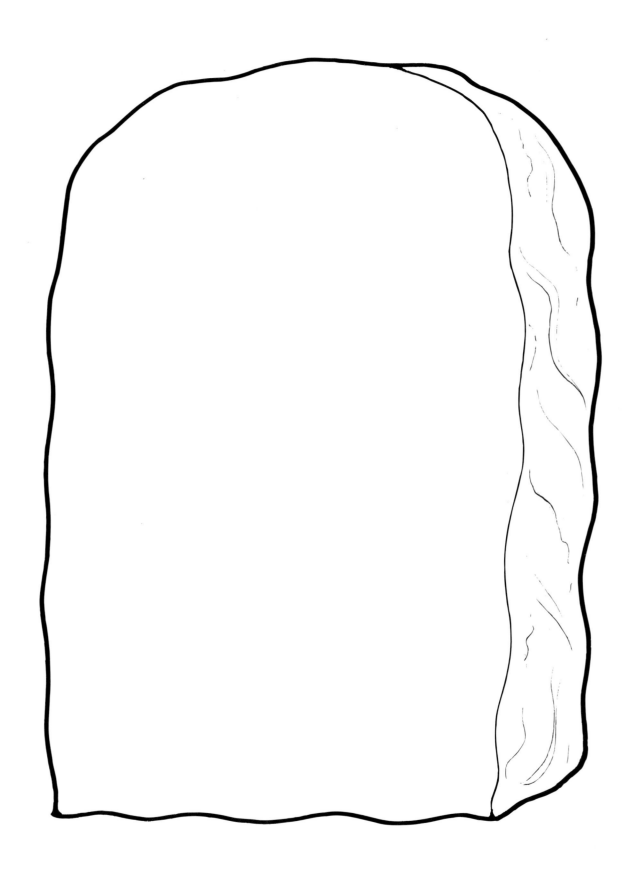

Use with *The Ten Commandments* bulletin board, page 14.

Use with *The Ten Commandments* bulletin board, page 14.

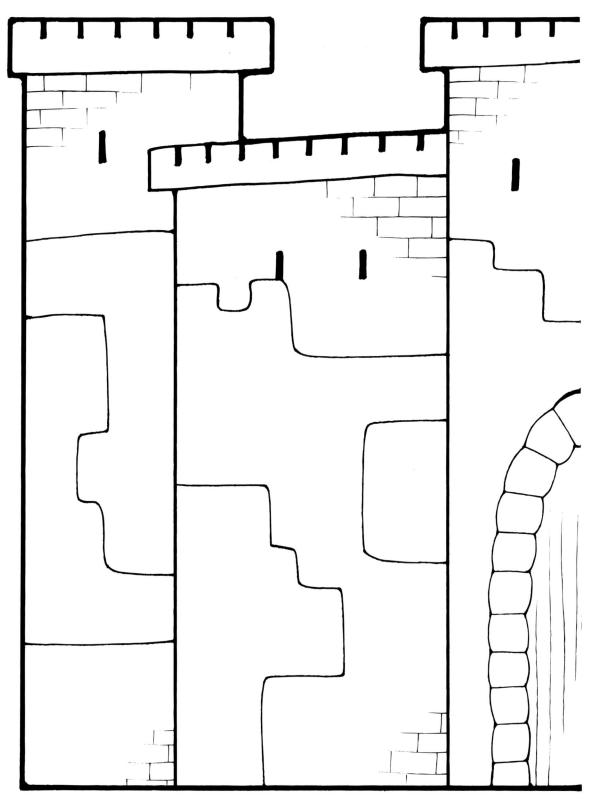

Use with *The Battle of Jericho* bulletin board, page 15.

Use with *The Battle of Jericho* bulletin board, page 15.

Use with *The Battle of Jericho* bulletin board, page 15.

Use with *The Sword of the Lord and Gideon* bulletin board, page 16.

Use with *The Sword of the Lord and Gideon* bulletin board, page 16.

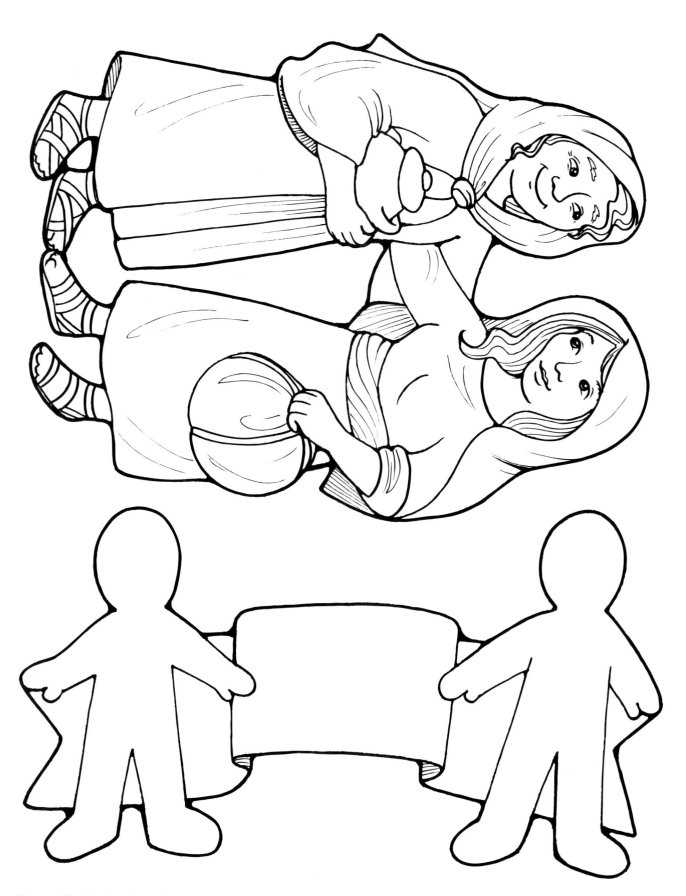

Use with the *Ruth and Naomi* bulletin board, page 17.

76

Use with the *David and Goliath* bulletin board, page 19.

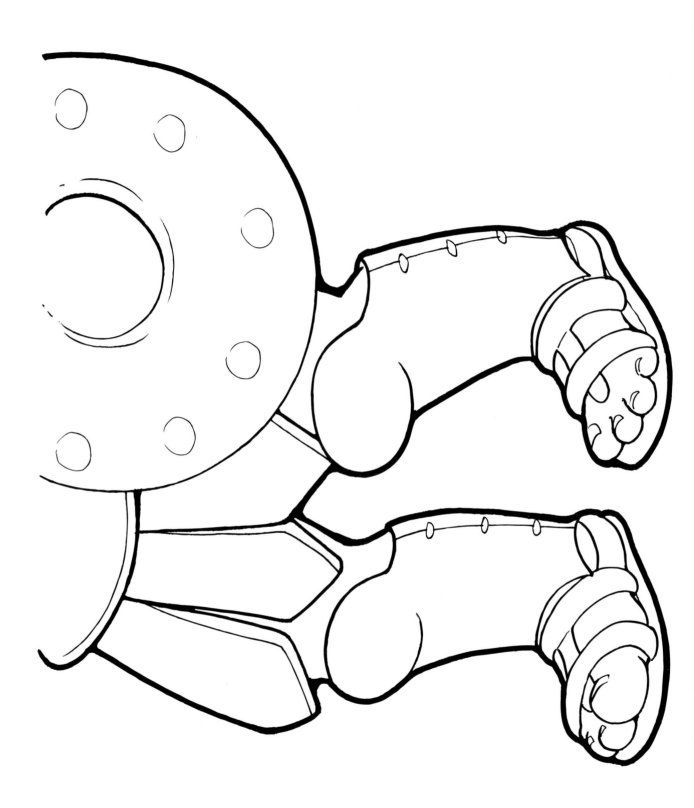

Use with the *David and Goliath* bulletin board, page 19.

Use with the *David and Goliath* bulletin board, page 19.

Use with the *Samuel and Eli* bulletin board, page 18.

 CD-204003 *Interactive Bible Story Bulletin Boards*

Use with the *Elijah and the Ravens* bulletin board, page 20.

Use with the *Proverbs* and *Saul's Conversion* bulletin boards, pages 23 and 47.

Use with *The Shepherd Psalm* bulletin board, page 22.

Use with the *Prince of Peace* and *Comfort for God's People* bulletin boards, pages 24-25.

 CD-204003 *Interactive Bible Story Bulletin Boards*

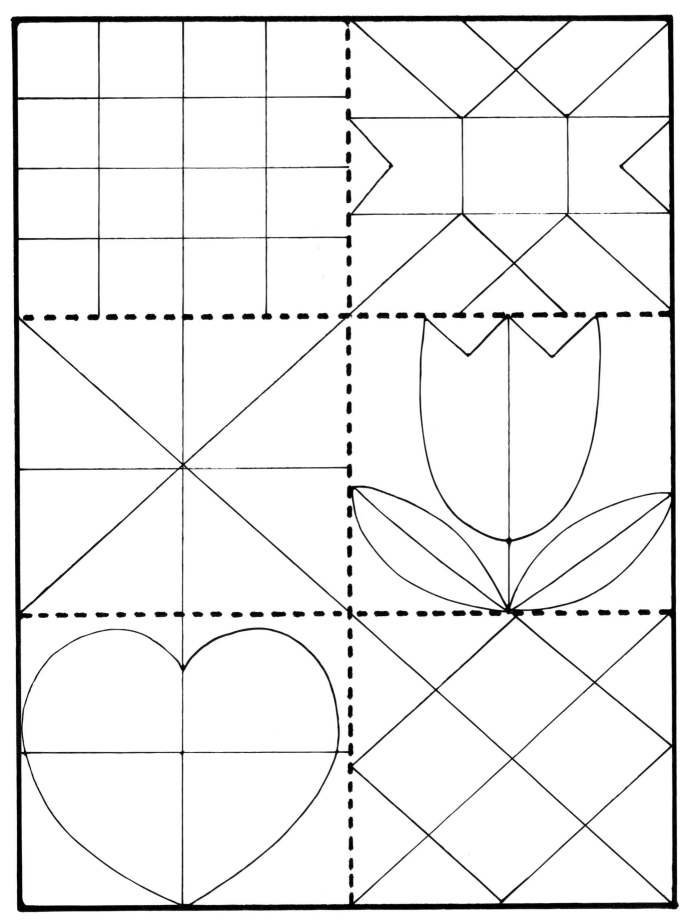

Use with the *Comfort for God's People* bulletin board, page 25.

 CD-204003 *Interactive Bible Story Bulletin Boards*

Use with the *Josiah and the Book of the Law* bulletin board, page 21.

 CD-204003 *Interactive Bible Story Bulletin Boards*

Use with the *Josiah and the Book of the Law* bulletin board, page 21.

Use with the *Writing on the Wall* bulletin board, page 26.

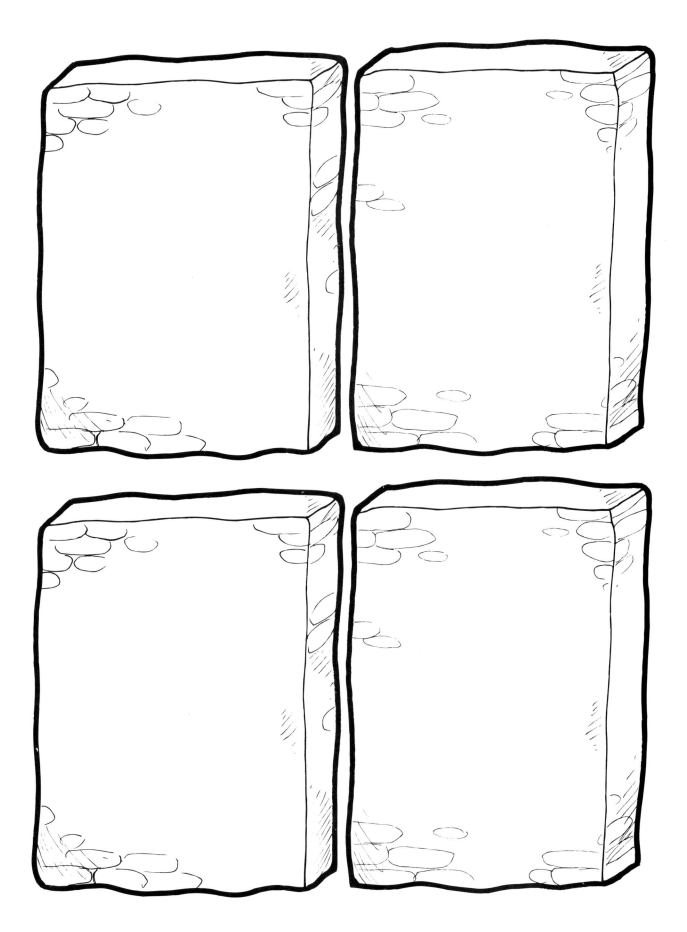

Use with the *Writing on the Wall* bulletin board, page 26.

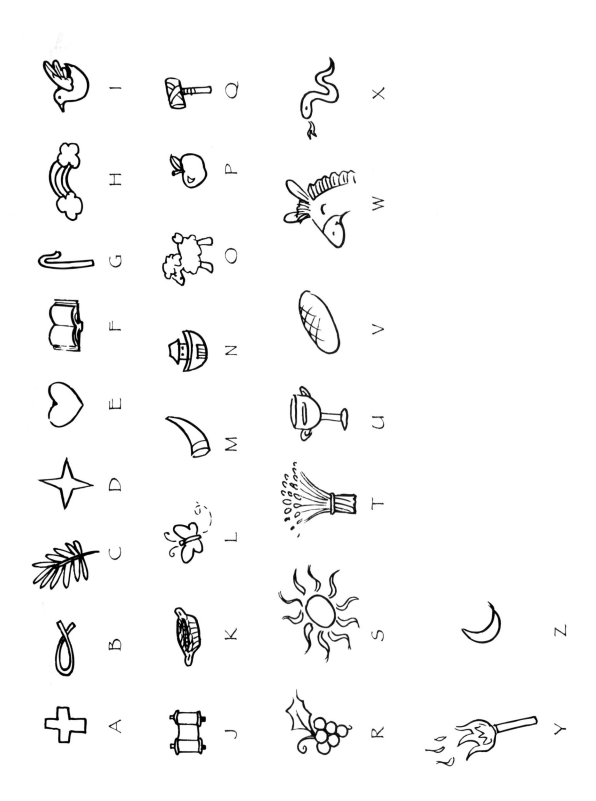

Use with the *Writing on the Wall* bulletin board, page 26.

CD-204003 *Interactive Bible Story Bulletin Boards*

Use with the *Daniel and the Lions' Den* bulletin board, page 27.

Use with the *Daniel and the Lions' Den*
bulletin board, page 27.

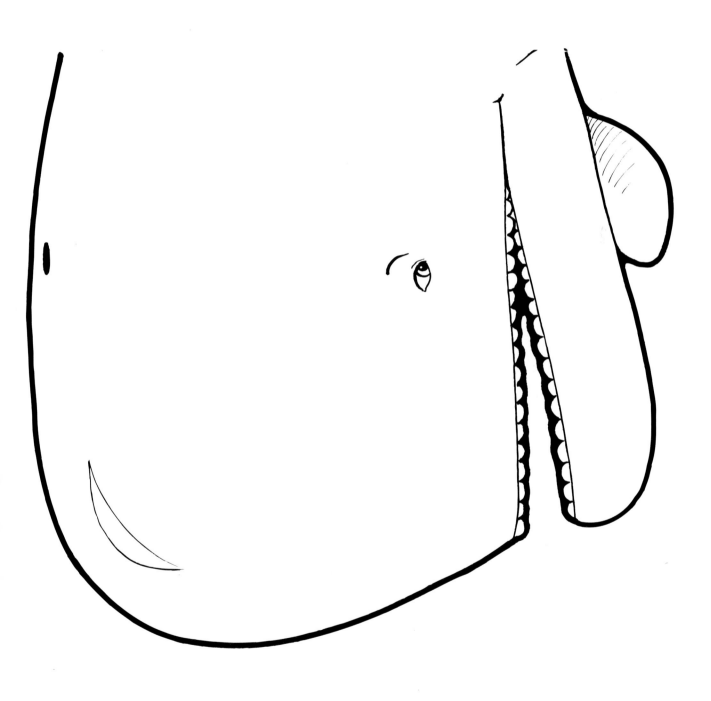

Use with the *Jonah and the Whale* bulletin board, page 28.

Use with the *Jonah and the Whale* bulletin board, page 28.

 CD-204003 *Interactive Bible Story Bulletin Boards*

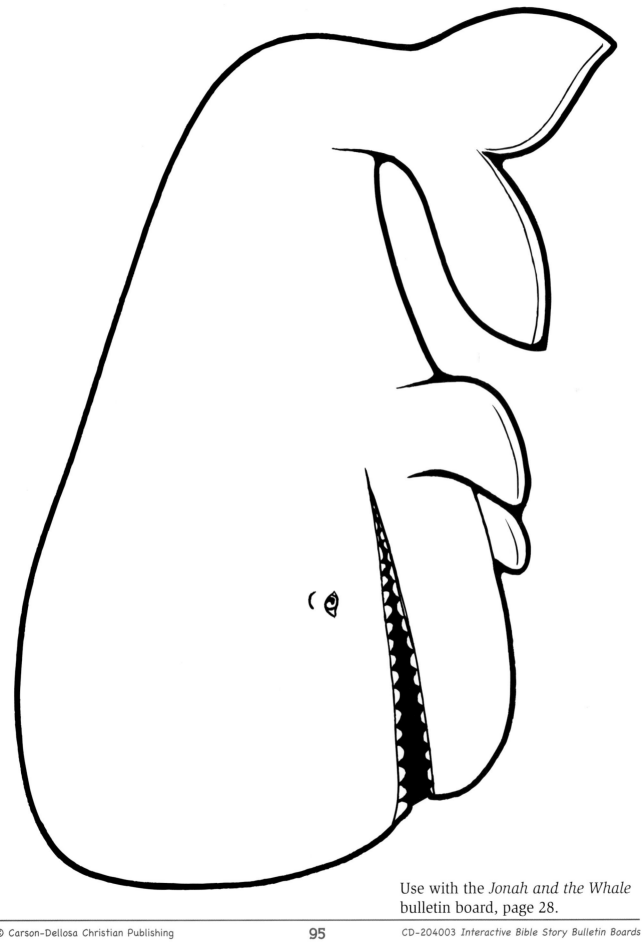

Use with the *Jonah and the Whale* bulletin board, page 28.

CD-204003 *Interactive Bible Story Bulletin Boards*

Use with the *Journey of the Magi* bulletin board, page 30.

Use with the *Journey of the Magi* bulletin board, page 30.

Use with the *Journey of the Magi* bulletin board, page 30.

Use with *The Lord's Prayer, Jesus and the Children,* and *Jesus' Humility* bulletin boards, pages 33, 42, and 51.

CD-204003 *Interactive Bible Story Bulletin Boards*

Use with *The Lord's Prayer,
Jesus and the Children, and
Jesus' Humility* bulletin
boards, pages 33 and 42.

 CD-204003 *Interactive Bible Story Bulletin Boards*

Use with the *Jesus and the Children* and *Jesus' Humility* bulletin boards, pages 42 and 51.

Use with *The Lord's Prayer* bulletin board, page 33.

CD-204003 *Interactive Bible Story Bulletin Boards*

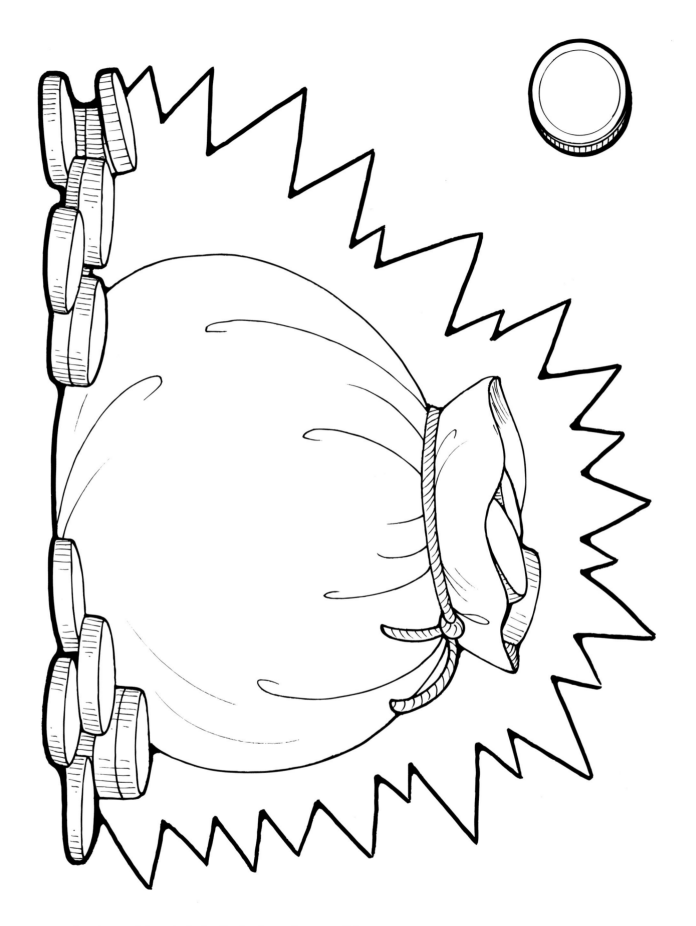

Use with *The Golden Rule* bulletin board, page 34.

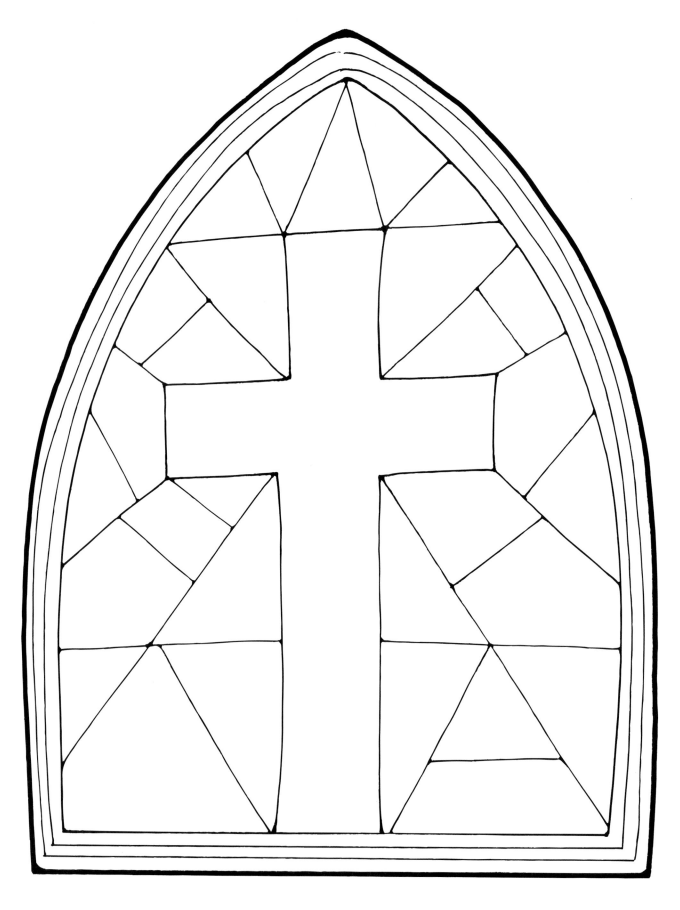

Use with the *Jesus and the Cross* bulletin board, page 45.

Use with *The Beatitudes* bulletin board, page 32.

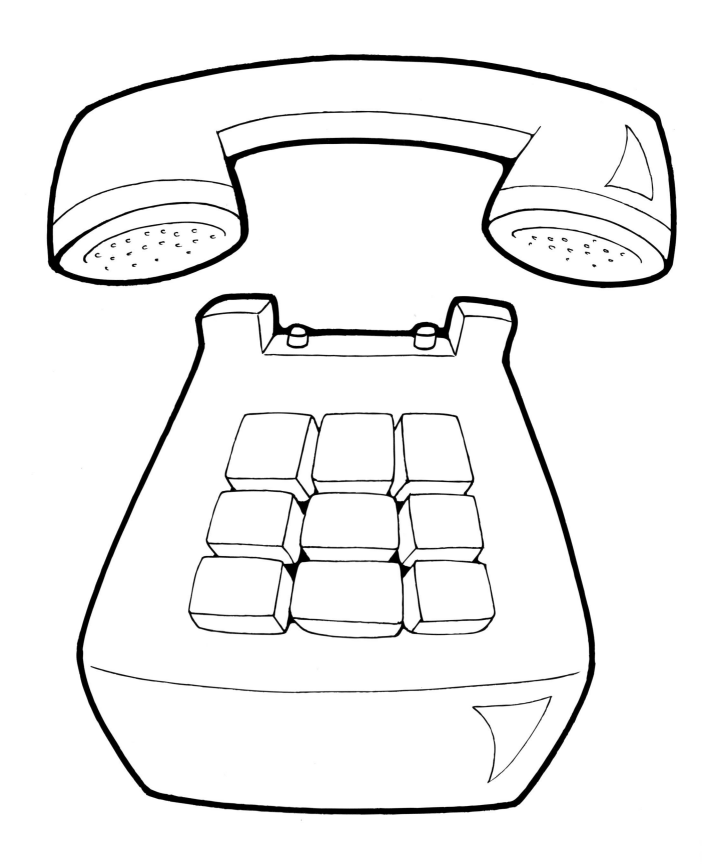

Use with the *Mary and Martha* bulletin board, page 40.

Use with *The Good Samaritan* and *Jesus and the Children* bulletin boards, pages 39 and 42.

Use with the *Jesus and the Children* and *Zacchaeus the Tax Collector* bulletin boards, pages 42-43.

Use with the *Jesus Is Born* bulletin board, page 29.

 CD-204003 *Interactive Bible Story Bulletin Boards*

Use with the *Jesus is Born* and *Parable of the Sower* bulletin boards, pages 29 and 36.

 CD-204003 *Interactive Bible Story Bulletin Boards*

Use with the *Parable of the Sower* bulletin board, page 36.

Use with the *Fishers of Men* and *Jesus Feeds the 5,000*, bulletin boards, page 31 and 37.
Use with the *Bread of Life* and *The Lost Son* bulletin boards, pages 38 and 41.

Use with *The Lost Son* bulletin board, page 41

Use with *The Lost Son* bulletin board, page 41.

Use with *The Lost Son* bulletin board, page 41.

Use with the *Jesus Lives!* bulletin board, page 46.

Use with the *Fishers of Men* bulletin board, page 31.

Use with the *Bread of Life* and *Fruit of the Spirit* bulletin boards, pages 38 and 49.

 CD-204003 *Interactive Bible Story Bulletin Boards*

Use with the *Jesus' Entry into Jerusalem* bulletin board, page 44.

Use with the *Woman at the Well* bulletin board, page 35.

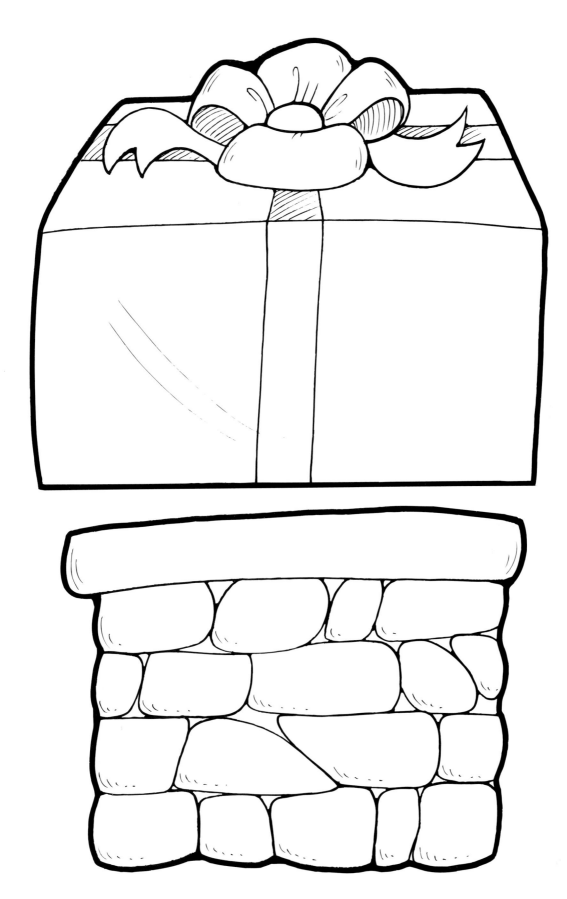

Use with the *Woman at the Well* bulletin board, page 35.
Use with the *Gracious Gifts* bulletin board, page 48.

Use with the *Bread of Life, Saul's Conversion,* and *Fruit of the Spirit* bulletin boards, pages 38, 47, and 49.

 CD-204003 *Interactive Bible Story Bulletin Boards*

Use with the *Saul's Conversion* bulletin board, page 47.

Use with the *Visions of Heaven* bulletin board, page 51.

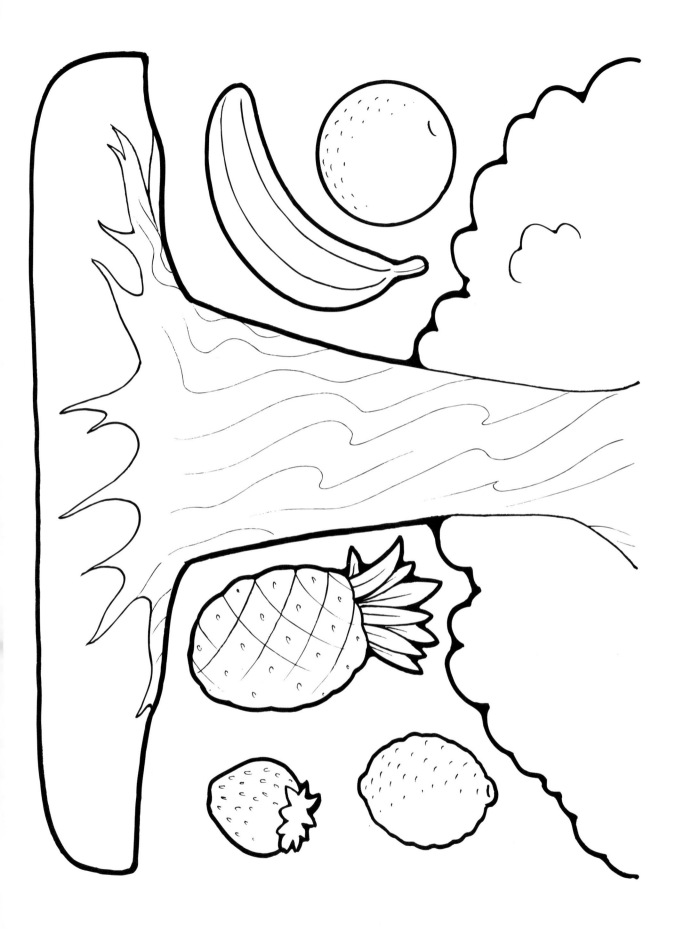

Use with the *Bread of Life* and *Fruit of the Spirit* bulletin boards, pages 38 and 49.

Use with the *Fruit of the Spirit* bulletin board, page 49.

 CD-204003 *Interactive Bible Story Bulletin Boards*

Use with the *Armor of God* bulletin board, page 50.

Use with the *Jesus' Humility* bulletin board, page 51.